ANIMALS UNDER THREAT

PEREGRINE FALCON

SAVED FROM EXTINCTION!

Mike Unwin

Heinemann Library
Chicago, Illinois

© 2004 Heinemann Library
a division of Reed Elsevier Inc.
Chicago, Illinois

Customer Service 888-454-2279

Visit our website at www.heinemannlibrary.com

Design: Jo Hinton-Malivoire and Tokay,
    Bicester, UK (www.tokay.co.uk)
Picture Research: Rosie Garai and Liz Eddison
Originated by Ambassador Litho Ltd.
Printed in China by WKT
Company Limited

08 07 06 05 04
10 9 8 7 6 5 4 3 2 1

Library of Congress Cataloging-in-Publication Data
Unwin, Mike.
  Peregrine falcon / Mike Unwin.
      p. cm. -- (Animals under threat)
Summary: Discusses the plight of peregrine falcons and why they are near extinction, as well as some of the ways humans can help.
Includes bibliographical references and index.
  ISBN 1-4034-4862-0 (HC), 1-4034-5436-1 (Pbk.)
  1. Peregrine falcon--Juvenile literature. [1. Peregrine falcon. 2.Falcons. 3. Endangered species.] I. Title. II. Series.
QL696.F34U58 2003
598.9'6--dc22

                              2003016142

Acknowledgments
The author and publishers are grateful to the following for permission to reproduce copyright material: p. 4 Eric and David Hosking/Corbis; p. 5 Wendy Dennis/FLPA; pp. 6, 37 Wendy Shattil and Bob Rozinski/Oxford Scientific Films; p. 7 W. Wisniewski/FLPS; p. 8 Galen Rowell/Corbis; p. 9 Gianni Dagli Orti/Corbis; p. 10 Francois Gohier/Ardea; p. 11 Steven Kaufman/Bruce Coleman; p. 13 John Watkins/FLPA; p. 14 N. N. Birks/Ardea; p. 15 Stephen Dalton/NHPA; p. 16 Piers Cavendish/Ardea; p. 17 James De Bounevialle/Alamy; p. 19 NHPA; p. 20 Alan Williams/NHPA; p. 21 David Hollands/FLPA; p. 22 Richard and Julia Kemp/SAL/Oxford Scientific Films; p. 23 David Hosking/FLPA; p. 24 Steven Kaufman/Corbis; p. 25 Eric and David Hosking; FLPA; p. 26 Ian Beames/Ardea; p. 27 Annie Griffiths Belt/Corbis; p. 28 R. I. Smith/Ardea; p 29 G. I. Bernard/NHPA; p. 30 Minden Pictures/FLPA; p. 31 A. Montemaggiori/Panda/FLPA; p. 32 Adam Woolfitt/Corbis; p. 33 Gary Roberts/Rex; p. 34 Bob Gibbons/Ardea;p. 35 James D Morgan/Rex; p. 36 M. Watson/Ardea; p. 38 Martin Dohrn/Nature Picture Library; p. 39 Corbis/FLPA; p. 40 Jean-Paul Ferrero/Ardea; p. 42 Martin Perry; p. 43 Natural Exposures.

Cover photograph reproduced with permission of Eric and David Hosking/Corbis.

Special thanks to Dr. David Willard, Collection Manager/Birds, at the Field Museum in Chicago for his review of this book.

The author would like to thank the following people for their help and advice in the preparation of this book: Jack Cafferty, The Peregrine Fund; Graham Elliot, Royal Society for the Protection of Birds; Dr Andrew Jenkins, Percy FitzPatrick Institute, University of Cape Town; John Pawsey.

Disclaimer
All the Internet addresses (URLs) given in this book were valid at the time of going to press. However, due to the dynamic nature of the Internet, some addresses may have changed, or sites may have ceased to exist since publication. While the author and publishers regret any inconvenience this may cause readers, no responsibility for any such changes can be accepted by either the author or the publisher.

The paper used to print this book comes from sustainable resources.

Some words are shown in bold, **like this.** You can find out what they mean by looking in the glossary.

Contents

The Peregrine Falcon

The peregrine falcon is one of the fastest and most skillful hunters in the animal kingdom. Its appearance in the sky can strike fear into other birds. People have admired its hunting abilities for thousands of years. Unfortunately, people have not always treated the peregrine with the care and respect that it deserves. During the 20th century, its population fell so rapidly all over the world that it became an **endangered species.**

This book tells the story of the peregrine falcon, explaining how it lives, why it became threatened, and how it has since made a remarkable recovery.

Raptors

Like all falcons, the peregrine is a **raptor,** a bird of prey. Like most birds of prey, it lives by hunting, killing, and eating other animals. It has special tools for this job, including a hooked bill for tearing flesh, powerful **talons** for holding its victims, and excellent eyesight for spotting **prey.** Eagles, vultures, kites, hawks, and harriers are also raptors. Falcons wings are more pointed than other raptors' wings. This wing shape gives them great flying skills. Many birds, including the peregrine, catch their prey as they are flying. Falcons also have a notch in the upper half, or mandible, of the bill. This is called the tomial tooth. It helps them to kill and pull apart their prey.

▲ The hooked bill and sharp claws of a peregrine falcon show that it is a bird of prey.

▶

The African pygmy falcon is a fierce little hunter that can catch other birds as big as itself.

Other falcons

There are over 50 different species of falcon. The largest is the gyrfalcon of Arctic regions, which measures up to 24 inches (60 centimeters) long. Among the smallest is the tiny African pygmy falcon which, at 7 inches (19 centimeters), is only the size of a starling. The Mauritius kestrel, found only on the island of Mauritius in the Indian Ocean, is one of the rarest birds in the world. There are no more than 400 individuals left.

The peregrine in close-up

The peregrine is one of the largest and most powerful falcons, with a compact body, big chest, and broad shoulders. As with many raptors, the female (known as the falcon) is bigger than the male (known as the tiercel). The female averages 18 to 20 inches (45 to 50 centimeters) in length and 2.4 pounds (1.1 kilograms) in weight. The male averages 15 to 18 inches (39 to 45 centimeters) and 23 ounces (650 grams). Both the male and female have blue-gray upperparts and creamy white underparts. The breast and belly are marked with a pattern of thin black horizontal lines. The face has a black "moustache" on either side of the hooked bill. The bare skin around the eye and at the base of the bill is bright yellow, and so are the feet. Young birds are more brown in color, with streaks rather than lines underneath. In flight, a peregrine's shape can look a little like a boat anchor, with its pointed wings swept back on either side of its short, straight tail.

Peregrine Country

This map shows the worldwide distribution of the peregrine falcon.

N

☐ Resident all-year round
☐ Summer breeding range
☐ Winter nonbreeding range

The peregrine falcon is one of the most widespread birds in the world. It makes its home on every continent except Antarctica. You will find nesting peregrines (the breeding range) on over 40 percent of the earth's land surface. However, this does not mean that the peregrine is common. In every part of the world its numbers are low and its breeding sites are scattered.

A suitable habitat

Around the world, the peregrine is found in many different **habitats,** including the Arctic **tundra,** the African grasslands, and islands in the Pacific Ocean. Good peregrine habitats all provide the falcon with three important things: wide open country for easy hunting, a good supply of other birds for **prey,** and steep cliffs (or even buildings) for nesting. In northern Europe and North America, peregrines tend to prefer sea cliffs or mountainous regions. In the deserts of Asia or the African grasslands, they choose areas with deep ravines or river gorges. Peregrines do not generally like forests, since a dense cover of trees makes it harder to spot and catch their prey.

This canyon in Colorado offers perfect habitat for a peregrine.

Worldwide wanderers

The peregrine gets its name from the Latin word *peregrinus*, which means "wanderer." During winter many peregrines wander far from their breeding sites in search of food. Some individuals may travel over 12,000 miles (20,000 kilometers) a year, crossing continents and turning up in all kinds of unlikely places. One was even seen taking a rest on a boat in the middle of the Atlantic Ocean!

Peregrines from the mountains come down to the coastal lowlands where there are more birds to hunt. Birds from northern climates fly south to regions where the weather is milder. Those from the far north make the longest journeys. For example, peregrines that breed in the American Arctic spend the winter in Central and South America. These long-distance northerners often pass the local peregrine populations as they fly south.

Cassin's falcon is a subspecies of peregrine from South America.

Peregrine variations

The peregrine is a unique **species** of bird. Like all species, it has its own scientific name, *Falco peregrinus*. However, the peregrine has spread so widely around the world that over time it has **evolved** into at least eighteen different regional forms, or **subspecies**. Each subspecies looks slightly different and has been given a third part to its scientific name. In North America there are three subspecies. *Falco peregrinus anatum* is the most common in much of the United States. *Falco peregrinus pealei* is larger and darker and is found along the northwest Pacific coast. *Falco peregrinus tundrius* is paler and is found in northern Canada.

In the middle of the 20th century, the world's peregrine population fell so low that in many areas the bird was in danger of **extinction.** The decline was worst in the United States. In the early 1960s, only 39 breeding pairs were recorded in the whole country. At about the same time, the population in the United Kingdom fell to only 360 pairs. In many other parts of the world, people also reported that peregrines were disappearing. Today, thanks to **conservation** efforts, numbers have risen again. There are now over 4,000 breeding pairs in North America, over 5,000 in Australia and over 6,000 in Europe.

Counting peregrines

It is impossible to calculate exactly how many peregrines there are worldwide. The best way to measure the breeding population is to keep a watch on nest sites, because peregrines usually return to the same site every year. Measuring the nonbreeding population is much harder. Young peregrines keep traveling until they settle down to breed. Collecting information is easier in developed countries, such as the United States, where nest sites are well-known and there are plenty of observers. In more remote parts of the world, scientists often just have to make estimates.

Scientists can put leg bands with numbers on young peregrines. This helps to track their progress when they leave the nest.

The world famous Bayeux Tapestry was embroidered over 900 years ago. In this section, you can spot a peregrine perched on a horseman's wrist.

Keeping tabs

Monitoring the movements of peregrines also gives scientists an idea of their numbers. Young falcons in the nest can be fitted with leg bands or colored wing tags. This allows scientists to recognize a bird if it is seen or recaptured somewhere else. Scientists can also track a peregrine's movements by satellite. A small transmitter fitted to its back gives off electronic signals. The signals are read by a satellite. The signals tell exactly where the bird is at any time. Bands, tags, and satellite transmitters do not harm the falcon.

Peregrines through the ages

Historical records show that the peregrine has been known to people for thousands of years. The ancient Egyptians and Chinese used peregrines for hunting as early as 2000 B.C. Peregrine bones have been uncovered among the excavations of 9th-century Viking homes in Scotland. The earliest written record of a peregrine nest dates from 1241, when King Henry III of England presented young falcons as gifts to a friend. These old records can sometimes be helpful to modern scientists, by giving an idea of where the birds lived in the past.

Watching the skies

Every spring and autumn, migrating **raptors,** including peregrines, gather in large numbers at key points on their journey, such as at sea crossings or mountain passes. Here, observers can count the birds as they pass overhead. This gives some idea of the number of peregrines in a particular area. It may also reveal how many young birds have been successfully raised that year. Well known raptor watch points include Hawk Mountain in the United States and the Straits of Gibraltar in the Mediterranean.

The peregrine falcon is the jet fighter plane of the bird world. Its muscular body is unusually heavy for a bird of its size and is built for speed and power in the air. The long wings are wide at the base and narrow at the tip. This allows the peregrine to accelerate quickly with short, shallow flaps. The wing tips can be folded back for flying fast or spread wide for braking and turning. The tail is usually kept neatly folded so that it does not catch the wind and slow the falcon down. But the tail feathers can be spread wide to brake suddenly, or to catch the warm air currents when the peregrine is soaring high.

A peregrine spreads its tail wide to make a high speed turn in midair.

Deadly weapons and useful tools

A peregrine's deadly hunting weapons are its powerful feet and hooked bill. In flight, the feet are tucked neatly out of the way until the peregrine reaches its target. Then the long legs stretch out to strike. The long toes with sharp **talons** are used to catch the **prey** in midair. If the prey falls, the talons pin it to the ground while the falcon uses its bill to deliver a killing neck bite. After a kill, the bill and talons are still useful tools. The talons hold the prey steady, while the bill plucks out the prey's feathers and tears off strips of flesh to swallow.

One vision

A peregrine has much more powerful eyesight than people do. It can detect movement and colors much better than people can. It is even said to be able to spot a pigeon at a distance of 5 miles (8 kilometers). Like all hunters, a peregrine's eyes are positioned toward the front of its head to give it binocular vision. This means that its two eyes form a single image of its target. Binocular vision allows a peregrine to judge distance very accurately when it is flying at high speed.

Speed limit

It is hard to measure the speed of a **stooping** peregrine. Scientists once estimated a top speed of 217 miles (350 kilometers) per hour. Today they know that this is impossible. Air pressure at this speed would make any bird unconscious. The peregrine's maximum is now thought to be about 150 miles (240 kilometers) per hour. In level flight, the fastest recorded bird is the eider duck, at 47 miles (75 kilometers) per hour.

A peregrine's eyes face forward so that it can focus clearly on its prey.

A Supreme Hunter

The peregrine falcon is exclusively a hunter. Its survival depends entirely upon catching and killing other birds. Powerful hunters like the peregrine are known as **apex predators.** This means that they sit right at the top of the **food web** and have little fear of other hunters. Below the peregrine in the food pyramid are the many other kinds of birds on which it feeds and the plants and animals the prey **species** eat.

Feathered food

Peregrines feed almost entirely upon birds. They can catch a wide variety of species, from tiny 0.35-ounce (10-gram) songbirds to big 3-pound (1.5-kilogram) grouse. In most areas their favorite **prey** is medium-sized birds such as pigeons, ducks, and game birds. Peregrines can kill birds as large or larger than themselves, including herons and black-backed gulls. But they cannot easily carry anything that weighs more than they do.

Their choice of prey also depends upon where they live. In some regions, peregrines feed mostly on one particular kind of bird that is common. The main food of peregrines on the Queen Charlotte Islands in the northeast Pacific Ocean is a small seabird called the marbled murrelet, which lives in huge colonies on the coast.

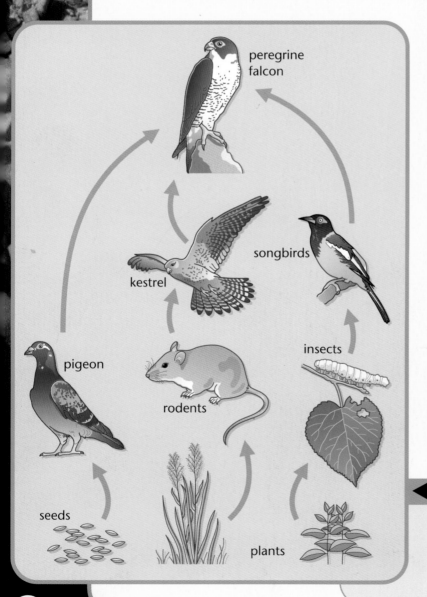

peregrine falcon

songbirds

kestrel

pigeon

rodents

insects

seeds

plants

In a food web, each animal or plant is eaten by the animal or plant above it. The arrows show how food energy passes up the food web to the peregrine at the top.

Pigeons are the favorite prey of peregrines in many parts of the world.

A wider diet

Although the peregrine generally feeds on common prey, such as pigeons, it is not picky about what it eats and will grab any hunting opportunity that comes along. Its more surprising victims include other hunters such as kestrels and even owls. In some places, including parts of Texas, peregrines have learned how to catch bats when they come out of their caves at dusk.

Small ground mammals, such as rabbits or voles, are also occasionally on the peregrine's menu, although it cannot catch prey on the ground as easily as in the air. One peregrine in Alaska was even seen to catch a salmon as it leaped out of the water.

Predators on peregrines

Occasionally the peregrine finds itself hunted rather than hunting. In the air, no bird is fast or powerful enough to threaten it, except perhaps another peregrine. But a larger **predator** can catch a peregrine when it is **roosting**. The European eagle owl and the American great horned owl have both been known to prey upon roosting peregrines at night. Foxes, raccoons and pine martens may also raid peregrine nests and kill the young. However, during the day the adult falcons will drive away these predatory mammals.

A pigeon is seldom fast enough to escape from a peregrine.

Just like a cheetah on the African plains, the peregrine uses speed and surprise to catch its **prey.** It first spots its target by looking out from a high perch or by soaring up and scanning below. Then the attack starts from above. The peregrine climbs high in the sky, folds back its wings, and falls toward its prey in a long, slanting dive, getting faster all the time. This dive is called a **stoop.** By the time the prey notices the danger, it is often too late to escape. The peregrine strikes it with a massive blow, using both feet clenched into fists. The force of the impact sometimes kills the prey outright, or leaves it fatally injured.

Claiming the prize

After a strike the peregrine quickly swoops around to get its prey. It either catches it as it tumbles through the air or follows it down to the ground. It then carries its prize back to the nest, or a favorite eating spot, to enjoy its meal in peace. Unwanted parts, such as the head, may be removed on the way. Large prey that is too heavy to carry is eaten where it has fallen. A feeding peregrine spreads its wings protectively over its kill in a posture known as **mantling.** It plucks out the feathers before tearing into the soft flesh beneath.

Peregrine feeding signs

A peregrine uses a regular feeding spot such as a favorite rock or tree stump. This is known as a plucking post. Here you will find the remains of its kills. Among the litter of feathers, the victim's wings are usually left intact and still attached to each other. There may also be **regurgitated** pellets that contain feathers, feet, and pieces of bone. A sure sign that the killer was a peregrine and not, for example, a fox, are V-shaped notches in the breast bone where the flesh was torn away with the peregrine's hooked bill.

A peregrine plucked the feathers from this curlew before starting to feed.

Hunting tactics

A peregrine's attack does not always succeed. If birds spot the danger coming, they may try to escape by flying high above the falcon, diving into the water, or ducking into the tree canopy. About 60 percent of a peregrine's hunting attempts are successful. However, peregrines often seem to pursue prey for fun, so it is not always clear when they are hunting seriously. If the prey avoids the first stoop, the falcon may rise again and repeat the dive, or it may roll over and try to strike the target from below. Sometimes a peregrine will chase after its prey and try to grab it from behind, particularly if the prey is tired or injured. Peregrines often approach from out of the glare of the sun or from around a corner of a cliff, to surprise their prey. They also sometimes hunt in pairs, one driving prey towards the other.

The peregrine has never been a very common bird. This is because good **habitat** is not easy to find. Even in the right habitat, each breeding pair needs plenty of space. This space is called a **territory.** Like most **apex predators,** peregrine territories are widely spaced out so that the falcons do not compete with one another. The size of a territory varies according to the food supply. In areas where there is plenty of **prey,** peregrines may nest within 0.6 miles (1 kilometer) of each other. In places with less prey, each territory may be over 12 miles (20 kilometers) from end-to-end. Hunting peregrines sometimes fly over one another's territories in their search for food. But their nest sites are always set well apart.

Peregrines need a large territory with lots of open space for hunting.

The wanderers return

Some peregrines remain in one place all year, while others wander widely during the winter. By early spring, every peregrine must have secured a territory in order to start breeding. Young birds, born a couple of years before, may have to find a new place of their own. Older birds usually return to the same territory year after year. Many territories never change. Some peregrines are said to have **ancestral homes.** A nest site on the British island of Lundy, which was occupied by peregrines 700 years ago, is still being used by peregrines today. During the late 20th century, as peregrine populations began to recover around the world, many peregrines returned to nest sites that had been empty for over 50 years.

Neighborhood watch

Peregrines will not put up with intruders in their territory. They regularly patrol the neighborhood and drive away unwelcome visitors with dive-bombing attacks. Their targets include other large **raptors,** such as eagles, that compete with the peregrine for food and may also threaten the nest. They also attack other peregrines. Two rival falcons may lock **talons** in a fierce midair fight. Sometimes they even continue their battle on the ground below. The intruder usually loses the battle, because a falcon defending its territory will fight the hardest.

Eternal enemies

Around the west coast of the United Kingdom, the peregrine's greatest rival is the raven. This is a large species of crow that shares the peregrine's habitat and uses similar nest sites on cliffs. These two birds are very unfriendly neighbors, and they fight whenever one comes too close to the other's nest. Their midair battles often involve spectacular flying **displays,** with each bird trying to get above the other. When attacked by the faster falcon, the larger raven flips over in the air to defend itself with its feet.

On sea cliffs, ravens compete fiercely with peregrines for the best nest sites.

Peregrines are monogamous. This means that each bird usually has just a single mate and that the pair stays together until one partner dies. Some pairs may separate during winter, with each bird traveling on its own in search of food. In spring, however, they return to the nest site to prepare for breeding. Sometimes both birds arrive together, but often one bird, usually the male, arrives first and waits for its mate. While waiting, the male flies around his **territory,** calling loudly so that the female will not miss him when she turns up.

Flights of fancy

When both the male and female falcon are back in their territory, they go through a **courtship** routine in order to get to know each other again. This process takes a few weeks. At first the two birds seem shy, and just perch quietly a short distance apart. Soon the male gathers confidence. He starts to perform **display** flights to impress the female—diving, rolling, and looping the loop in front of her while calling loudly. The female often joins him. The two birds spiral high up into the air together then dive down again. The male also brings back **prey** as a gift to the female, who may fly out to collect it from him in midair.

Once the two falcons have become used to each other again, they spend more time together on the cliff ledge and perch side by side. The female starts to practice making nest **scrapes** with her feet. The pair display to each other, ducking their heads and bowing while calling loudly.

Mating

By eight weeks after the start of courtship, the two peregrines have built up a strong bond. Now they must mate so that the male can **fertilize** the unlaid eggs of the female. Again, a special ceremony takes place between the two birds. The male approaches the female with his wings raised and gives a high-pitched chittering call. The female answers with a wailing call. She ducks her head, leans forward, and twists her tail to one side to signal that she is ready. The male then climbs on top of the female with wings fluttering, and mating takes place. All the while, both birds continue to call loudly. Afterward, the male flies off in a slow, flapping display flight. The female fluffs out her feathers and settles back on the ledge. Mating only lasts a few seconds, but it is repeated three or four times an hour for several days.

Peregrine language

Peregrines use at least seven different calls to communicate. Each one has a different purpose. The cacking call is a harsh, chattering sound used to express aggression or alarm. The wailing call is a shrill, whining sound used when one peregrine wants something from its partner, such as food. The creaking call sounds like a rusty hinge. It is given by one peregrine to another during courtship displays.

During courtship, a male and female peregrine perch close together near their nest site. in this picture, the female bird is the one above.

A peregrine's nest is called an **eyrie.** It is usually found on a narrow ledge halfway up a steep cliff, where no **predator** can reach it. A good nesting ledge sticks out at least 20 inches (50 centimeters) from the cliff face to give the **fledglings** room to exercise. It also has a layer of soil, in which the parents hollow out a **scrape** for the eggs. Peregrines do not make a nest of sticks like many other birds. But this simple bowl—about 1 to 2 inches (3 to 5 centimeters) deep and 7 to 9 inches (17 to 22 centimeters) wide—stops their eggs from rolling off the ledge. One pair of peregrines may use several different scrapes on the same ledge over several years.

Eggs

The female peregrine lays her **clutch** of three to four eggs in early spring. In the Northern Hemisphere (North America, Europe, Asia) this means late March or early April. In the Southern Hemisphere (southern Africa, Australia, South America), this means late August to early September. The eggs are rounder than a hen's eggs and reddish-brown in color, patterned with white or reddish blotches. One egg is laid every 48 hours. It takes about one week for the female to lay the whole clutch.

Peregrines usually nest on a steep cliff ledge, where they dig a shallow scrape for their eggs.

Alternative nests

In a few places, peregrines do not nest on cliffs at all. In the forests of northeastern Europe and Australia, they regularly nest in tree tops. They often take over the old nests of crows, herons, or ospreys. In the bare Arctic **tundra**, where there are no trees or cliffs, peregrines nest in the grasses on the ground. Here, the wet, boggy land protects them from foxes and other ground predators.

Sitting

Once the last egg is laid, the parents take turns sitting on them. They are careful not to harm the eggs with their sharp **talons.** This is called **incubation.** Their warmth allows the **embryo** inside each egg to develop. A patch of bare skin on the adult's belly, known as the **brood** patch, helps transfer its body heat directly to the eggs.

The female does 75 percent of the incubation. She rolls the eggs over with her beak to make sure that each one gets an equal amount of warmth. While the female is sitting, the male hunts for food, which he brings back to the nest.

This unusual peregrine nest in Australia is located inside a hollow tree trunk.

Foster parents

Peregrines do not easily abandon their nests. If a female dies during the breeding season, the male will try to find a new mate to help with the incubation. The urge to incubate is so strong that a pair of peregrines have even been known to take over a clutch of abandoned kestrel eggs after losing their own. Scientists have also managed to persuade wild peregrines that have lost their own eggs to look after chicks that were hatched in captivity.

Growing Up

After 28 to 32 days of **incubation,** the eggs are ready to hatch. The chicks break through the shell from inside using an egg tooth, a small knob on the bill that all baby birds have for this purpose. Each chick takes about 72 hours to break free. About 48 hours usually pass between the hatching of the first and the last chick. Any egg damaged during incubation is usually eaten by the parents. They know that it will never hatch, so they no longer treat it as one of their own.

Early days

When peregrine chicks come out of the egg, they look nothing like their parents. Their eyes are closed, they have no **flight feathers,** and they are covered in fine white **down.** For the first sixteen days, they spend most of their time asleep under the warm body of one of their parents. This is called **brooding.** After four days, the chicks' eyes open for the first time. After eight days, they make their first feeble movements. Despite their helplessness, newly hatched chicks know how to eat. From the first day, the parents drop small pieces of meat into their gaping bills.

Peregrines tear off small pieces of food to feed to their chicks.

A young peregrine flaps its wings in preparation for its first flight.

Getting bigger

At three weeks, the chicks develop their first flight feathers and start to practice flapping their wings. This new activity gives them a big appetite. The parents are kept busy bringing a constant supply of **prey** to the nest, which the chicks gobble down in big chunks. At four weeks the parents stop brooding, and the chicks sleep alone rather than all together in a big huddle. Now they can stand up and **preen** their feathers. They can also squirt their droppings over the ledge to avoid messing up the nest.

Taking flight

After four weeks, the chicks start to shed their baby down, and their new feathers can be seen underneath. Now they are about the same size as their parents. They have all their flight feathers, and they are ready to leave the nest.

A young peregrine's first flight is usually at five to six weeks. Its parents encourage it by calling from a short distance away. They also leave food on a nearby perch. Young falcons take a while to master their flying skills. At first they crash-land clumsily wherever they find a perch. Gradually, they gain confidence and start to improve.

For a while, the young peregrines remain with their parents near the nest and practice their new skills. The adults provide hunting lessons by driving prey within close range. After about six weeks, the young falcons leave their parents and strike out alone.

Sport with Peregrines

Ancient art shows falcons being trained to hunt for people as early as 680 B.C. Today, the ancient sport of falconry is still being practiced. Its beginnings go back to the time of the early Egyptians and Chinese. It is thought to have reached Europe by the 3rd century A.D. Falconry demands great skill and dedication. The people who do it are known as falconers.

Prize falcon

Many different species of **raptors** are used in falconry. The peregrine has always been one of the most prized because of its hunting skills and because its mild nature makes it relatively easy to train.

In **medieval** England, a person's social position decided what kind of bird they could use. The common people used kestrels, while landowners used goshawks. Only nobles could hunt with the peregrine, which was said to be the falcon of kings.

A hood over the peregrine's eyes keeps it calm when not hunting. The falconer wears thick gloves for protection against the peregrine's

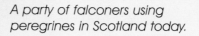
The art of falconry

The basic techniques of falconry have changed little over the centuries. Training starts soon after hatching. The falconer alone is responsible for all feeding and contact with the chick so that a close bond of trust develops between them. After four to five weeks (half the time it takes to train many other raptors), the young peregrine makes its first flight from the gloved fist of the falconer. At first it practices hunting on a lure. The lure is an artificial **prey** made of leather that the falconer whirls on the end of a rope. Soon it is ready to hunt real birds, such as partridges or ducks. The falconer trains the falcon to fly up high and wait, while dogs flush out the prey. The peregrine then **stoops** down to make a kill. After allowing the falcon to feed a little, the falconer then picks up the prey.

Falconry today

Today falconry is not as widespread as it was during medieval times. But there are still clubs and societies all over the world that keep the sport alive. Some people use falcons for hunting. Others just use them to perform in flying exhibitions. It is illegal to capture any bird of prey from the wild without a special license. So most falconers only use birds that have been bred in captivity. Each falcon must be legally registered with an identification band on its leg, just like the license plate on a car.

Sadly, many peregrines have been killed by people. This one was poisoned.

Beginning in the late 18th century, the widespread use of guns changed people's relationship with the peregrine in Europe. Shooting to catch game quickly became more popular than falconry. In many places, private land was set aside for shooting game birds such as pheasants and grouse. Landowners employed people called gamekeepers to protect game birds by getting rid of other **predators. Raptors** were now the enemy of the sportsman, and the peregrines were easy to kill because they always returned to the same nest sites.

From the late 1700s to the early 1900s, gamekeepers shot thousands of peregrines and destroyed the nests and eggs of many more. One record alone from an estate in Scotland shows that 1,799 raptors, including 98 peregrines, were killed in just four hunting seasons between 1837 and 1840.

A barrage of bullets

In other parts of the world, the peregrine has also suffered at the hands of hunters. It is often shot just for sport. In the Mediterranean region where hunters kill an estimated 500 million songbirds every year, the peregrine, like other raptors, often becomes a target. Although peregrines are internationally protected, many are still shot as they hunt along the cliffs along the Mediterranean Sea or migrate across the sea.

Catch the pigeon

The peregrine's appetite for pigeons has also led it into trouble. Beginning in 1890, the sport of pigeon racing became popular in both the United States and the United Kingdom. In this sport, people known as pigeon-fanciers release pet pigeons far from home and place bets on whose bird will get home first. These pigeons are known as racing or homing pigeons. Pigeon-fanciers were furious to discover that peregrines sometimes killed their valuable birds. Some took revenge by killing the falcons or destroying their nests.

Research has since shown that peregrines do not often kill racing pigeons. In 1999, only 3.5 percent of all racing pigeons flown in the United Kingdom were killed by peregrines. Many more simply got lost or were killed by colliding with windows or overhead wires. Today, however, some pigeon-fanciers continue to harm peregrines.

Misfortunes of war

The pigeon problem became more serious during World War II (1939–1945), when carrier pigeons were used by the British and U.S. forces to carry military messages across the English Channel to France. The British government needed to protect these vital wartime messengers. In 1940 it passed an emergency law to allow the destruction of peregrines and their nests in many coastal regions. Over 600 peregrines were killed during this period, and many eggs and young were destroyed. The law was canceled after the war, but by then the peregrine population in the United Kingdom had been reduced by more than half.

Racing pigeons are being released by pigeon-fanciers.

During the late 1940s and 1950s, the peregrine population fell sharply all over the world. At first, scientists could not understand why this was happening. By this time the peregrine had been declared a protected **species,** so hunting was no longer a big problem. The cause of the decline turned out to be something even more serious than hunting. The peregrine was dying out because of the chemicals that were being used on farmland; in particular, a **pesticide** called DDT.

What is DDT?

DDT (short for dichloro-diphenyl-trichloroethane) is one of group of chemical compounds known as organochlorines. These chemicals are used as pesticides to kill insects. They were first developed during World War II to protect troops in tropical countries from malaria, whch is a disease spread by mosquitoes. After the war, DDT was used on crops to protect them from insect pests. Huge areas of farmland across Europe and North America were sprayed. More crops were grown, but soon the wildlife began to suffer.

If its shell is too thin, a peregrine egg can be easily cracked by the sitting adults.

A chain of poison

DDT reached peregrines by making its way up the **food web.** Peregrines do not eat insects or crops, but they prey on other birds that do. When birds, fed on crops that had been sprayed with DDT, the chemical remained inside their bodies. Unlike more modern chemicals, it did not break down. The DDT was stored in the bird's flesh. If these birds were eaten by a peregrine, the chemical quickly passed from **prey** to **predator.** At each link in the food chain, the poison became stronger.

An aircraft is used to spray DDT over crops in Colombia, South America.

Broken eggs

At first it was not clear how DDT affected peregrines. The adult birds appeared to be healthy enough. But the clue was in the nest. Either their **broods** were much smaller (only one or two chicks instead of three or four), or their eggs never hatched. When scientists looked more closely at the damaged eggs, they discovered that the shells were too thin. The DDT was preventing the female peregrine's body from producing enough calcium. Calcium is a mineral needed to strengthen egg shells. With thin shells, the eggs simply cracked beneath the weight of the parent, or the **embryo** inside became overheated and died.

Tackling pesticide pollution

DDT was not the only villain, and the peregrine was not the only victim. Other forms of environmental pollution affected other birds. Industrial chemicals called PCBs (polychlorinated biphenyls) damaged the food chain at sea and affected fish eaters such as the brown pelican. By the early 1960s, people all over the world had begun to notice the disappearance of birds. In 1962 writer Rachel Carson wrote a famous book called *Silent Spring*, which drew attention to the problem. Governments took action. By the early 1970s most developed countries had placed strict controls on the use of organochlorines, including DDT. Peregrine numbers quickly began to recover.

Damaging Peregrine Habitats

The DDT disaster proved that to protect wildlife, people must also protect the wider environment in which the animals live. Living things are all connected by the **food web,** and damage in one place can quickly cause problems somewhere else. Today, there are still many threats to the environment that affect the peregrine in different ways.

Vanishing spaces

In winter, peregrines from upland regions visit lowland areas in search of food. American peregrines from the Rocky Mountains spend the winter along the Gulf of Mexico, where millions of waterbirds gather in the coastal wetlands. If these wetlands are drained for development, the bird flocks leave the area and the peregrines disappear with them. In the United Kingdom, peregrines hunt over the marshes near the Thames River in winter. In 2002 this area was proposed as the site of a new airport. An airpot would destroy the feeding grounds for thousands of birds and keep peregrines from their winter home. **Conservation** groups have campaigned against this plan.

Many peregrines visit wetlands during winter, where they hunt ducks and other water birds.

Trees in the way

Peregrines need plenty of open space for hunting, and they tend to avoid forests. In parts of northern Europe, commercial forests have been planted in regions where peregrines hunt. The thick growth of trees there discourages ground-nesting birds, such as grouse and golden plover, which are the peregrine's main **prey** in this region. If their food disappears, the peregrines have to go elsewhere.

Pollution at sea

Pollution at sea, such as oil or chemicals spilled from boats, can also affect the peregrine. In some areas, such as the Pacific northwest coast of Alaska, peregrines feed almost entirely on sea birds. If these birds are trapped in an oil spill, the peregrine's food source can become contaminated, or it may even completely disappear. In 1989 over 35,000 tons of crude oil spilled along the coast of Alaska from an oil tanker called the *Exxon Valdez*. Many animals, including sea otters and killer whales, were affected and over 250,000 seabirds died. Scientists are still assessing what impact this may have had on the peregrine's population.

▲ *Hunters in the Mediterranean shoot millions of birds; peregrines are at risk when they travel through this region.*

Keep off the cliffs

Peregrines nest on steep cliffs so that they can breed without being disturbed. Today, however, cliffs and gorges often attract people looking for adventurous sports such as rock climbing or hang gliding. Anyone who gets too close to a peregrine's nest may cause the birds to abandon the eggs. In most countries, climbers are now required by law to stay well clear of known peregrine nest sites.

Poaching

Toda, in most parts of the world, peregrines are protected by the law. There are strict penalties, including heavy fines and imprisonment, for anyone who breaks it. Unfortunately, because the peregrine is still rare, it is very valuable. Some people still go to great lengths to steal eggs or chicks from peregrine nests and sell them illegally.

In the past, collectors stole thousands of peregrine eggs for their display cases.

Egg collecting

Until the mid-20th century, collecting eggs was a popular hobby for people with an interest in birds. Collectors took eggs from wild birds nests to display in their own private collections. The eggs of rare **species,** such as the peregrine, were the most prized. Today, most people are more interested in watching wildlife, and egg collecting is now illegal. It still happens, but not as often. In 1991 at least 68 peregrine nests were raided in the United Kingdom. In 2001, just ten years later, only two thefts were recorded.

Wanted alive

Collecting peregrine eggs for display may no longer be in fashion, but live eggs and chicks are still stolen for illegal sale to falconers. **Legitimate** falconers are committed to the protection of wild peregrines, and they only use registered birds that have been bred in captivity.

But there is a thriving **black market** for wild falcons, particularly in the Middle East and Eastern Europe. A single peregrine chick can bring in more than $1,500. Peregrines are captured in one country and then smuggled into another to be sold. The birds often travel in terrible conditions, and many die on the journey.

Guarding peregrines

Many people work together to protect peregrines from nest thieves. In some places, volunteers keep a close watch on nest sites to check on the security of the birds. If thieves manage to raid the nests, special police wildlife officers are assigned to the case. With luck, they will catch the thieves and get the eggs or chicks before it is too late. If the thieves get away, customs officers are trained to spot anybody trying to smuggle falcons out of the country. In April 2002, the Eurogroup Against Bird Crime was formed. This organization enables European countries to fight together against the illegal trade in wild **raptors.**

This poster warns people that the birds' nests are being protected. SmartWater Technology is a company that develops security systems.

WARNING.

PROTECTED WILDLIFE IN THIS AREA
FORENSICALLY MARKED
BY
SMART WATER

Conservation Efforts

For many years the peregrine has been a victim of human carelessness and greed. People have hunted it, stolen its eggs, destroyed its nests, poisoned its food, and ruined its **habitat.** However, the peregrine has surprised many people by making a strong comeback from the dark days of the 1950s. Today, there are over 1,600 breeding pairs in the United States alone—40 times more than there were 50 years ago. In the United Kingdom, the population of over 1,300 pairs is more than three times larger than in the 1960s.

With a little help from your friends

The recovery of the peregrine happened because of the many scientists, volunteers, and **conservationists** who were determined that it should not disappear. Many organizations have played their part. In the United States, the Peregrine Fund helped to **reintroduce captive-bred** peregrines into the wild. In Canada, the Canadian Peregrine Foundation tracked migrating peregrines using satellite technology. In the United Kingdom, the Royal Society for the Protection of Birds (RSPB) secured protection for peregrine habitats. Larger organizations have helped by educating the public and talking to governments. Smaller ones have performed local tasks like taking care of injured birds or watching nests.

In the United Kingdom, the RSPB protects peregrine breeding habitats on bird reserves such as South Stack in Anglesey, Wales.

Spreading the word

Educating and informing the public is a top priority for all conservation organizations. They know that their work will not succeed without popular support. On June 30, 1981, Ed Koch, then the Mayor of New York City, declared Peregrine Day. This helped to put peregrines back on the map and gave people pride in their natural heritage. Today, falcon watch centers, nest site webcams, and falconry displays all help to raise public interest, knowledge, and support.

Raptor rescue

Trained experts can sometimes help a sick or injured peregrine recover and then return it to the wild. First, they take care of any injuries, such as a broken wing. Then, when the bird has healed, they help it to regain its flying skills. Finally, after a full recovery, they release it, leaving some food around to help it adjust gradually to life in the wild. This process is called rehabilitation.

▲ *This Australian peregrine has been shot. A volunteer is taking care of its injuries and helping it to recover.*

The long arm of the law

Today, the peregrine falcon is legally protected in most parts of the world. In the United States, it is classified as **endangered** by 32 states. In the United Kingdom, it is protected under the Wildlife and Countryside Act. In Europe it is listed under the European Union Wild Birds Directive. All these laws make it illegal to harm a peregrine or to be in possession of the bird, its eggs, or feathers without a license. The peregrine also falls under Appendix I of the Convention on International Trade in Endangered Species of Wild Fauna and Flora (CITES), which does not allow trade in wild peregrines or their eggs.

Reborn in the United States

By 1970 the peregrine appeared to be heading for **extinction** in the United States. It had vanished entirely from the East, while its numbers in the West had fallen by over 80 percent. **Conservationists** realized that something had to be done quickly before the falcon completely disappeared. At Cornell University, Dr. Tom Cade set up an organization called the Peregrine Fund. His plan was to **reintroduce** peregrines to their former homes by breeding them in captivity and then releasing them into the wild.

A glove puppet shaped like an adult peregrine hides the hand of the scientist feeding this chick.

Raised in a box

Before 1970, no captive peregrine had ever been successfully reintroduced to the wild. The Peregrine Fund developed a process that scientists now use to reintroduce **raptors** anywhere. To do this, they remove the first **clutch** of eggs from a wild peregrine's nest early in the breeding season, allowing her to lay a second clutch. The eggs of the first clutch are kept warm in an **incubator** until hatching. Then the **hatchlings** are spoon-fed every 3 to 4 hours for about three weeks.

The young peregrines are then shut into boxes, called hack boxes. These are placed on a ledge in the peregrine's natural **habitat.** Food is supplied through a long tube so the falcons learn to stop depending on humans. After four weeks, the chicks' legs have grown and each one is fitted with an identification leg band. After eight weeks, the hack boxes are opened and the young birds fly free. This is known as hacking out. Soon the peregrines leave the area. If they return, they can quickly be identified by their bands.

This young American peregrine will soon be released from the hack box to discover its new home.

Bringing peregrines home

In its first 25 years, the Peregrine Fund released over 4,000 young peregrines in 28 states. Many returned to their release sites to breed. In this way, new populations of peregrines gradually began to resettle their former homes. By the 1980s, peregrine falcons were once again breeding in the wild in the eastern United States. Similar successful programs took place in the Pacific Northwest and California. Meanwhile, the peregrine populations in Arizona and Utah began to recover naturally. In just 30 years, the U.S. population rose from 39 known pairs to over 1,500. This was the first nationwide recovery of an **endangered species** in the United States. Other groups soon learned from the Peregrine Fund. The Canadian Wildlife Service released over 4,000 falcons in a 20-year period ending in 1996. Results now show that the Canadian peregrine population is also recovering well.

Visit the Peregrine Fund

Today, the Peregrine Fund is based at the World Center for Birds of Prey in Boise, Idaho. Here, visitors can enjoy many exhibitions and activities. The work of the Fund has now expanded to include many other raptor conservation projects around the world. However, it still relies upon the hard work and dedication of volunteers and contributions of money from members of the public.

City Falcon

As the peregrine's numbers have recovered around the world, it has started to find a home in the city. Bridges, skyscrapers, and other tall buildings offer nest sites that are just like cliffs. Pigeons, starlings and other urban birds provide a ready supply of food.

Cities around the world

Cities are not an entirely new home for peregrines. One famous **eyrie** on the Sun Life Building in Montreal, Canada, was occupied every year from 1936 until 1952. But in the United States, the number of urban nest sites has been boosted by the **captive-release** program. The first nesting peregrines in New York City were two pairs that nested on the Throgs Neck and Verrazano Narrows bridges in 1983. Birds now nest in over 20 other U.S. cities, including Chicago and San Francisco. In other cities around the world, peregrines have discovered urban nest sites for themselves. In 2000, London's first breeding pair produced young on Battersea Power Station, overlooking the Thames River.

A helping hand

Skyscraper ledges seem to make perfect peregrine nest sites. **Predators** cannot reach them, and they command a wide view over the city for spotting **prey.** Unfortunately there is a problem. With no layer of soil on the ledge, the peregrine cannot dig a nest **scrape.** This puts the eggs at risk of rolling off. Also, some ledges are too narrow for the growing chicks, and young peregrines often crash land in the middle of busy streets.

To give city peregrines a helping hand, scientists put nest boxes on likely ledges. Each box has three sides, a layer of gravel for the scrape, and is wide enough for a growing **brood.** In some places, volunteers keep a constant watch on the nest while the **fledglings** are learning to fly. Any fledgling that ends up on the street can then be rescued.

From the top of a skyscraper, a peregrine can scan for prey right across the city.

This city peregrine is eating a duck called a wigeon, caught on a hunting trip outside town.

Poles and pyramids

Skyscrapers are not the only human-made structures that provide good nest sites. In some places peregrines use electricity poles, while in others they breed on tall industrial chimneys. And peregrines do not always choose modern buildings. One of the best known peregrine eyries in the United Kingdom was on Salisbury Cathedral, built in the 13th century. Peregrines used it for many years between the 1860s and 1950s. In Spain and Germany peregrines have often nested in ruined castles. In Egypt peregrines have even bred on the great pyramids, which are over 4,000 years old!

Eating out

In 1999 a study of peregrines nesting in Bristol, in the United Kingdom, showed that much of their prey came from outside the city. This included rural birds, such as teals, green woodpeckers, and partridges.

39

The Future for Peregrine Falcons

Today the peregrine falcon's future looks much safer than it did 50 years ago. It has recovered well since its low point in the mid 20th century. Populations in many places are now at their highest in over 100 years. **Eyries** that had long been empty are once again being used. By nesting in cities, the peregrine has also shown that it can adapt to changes in its environment. In 1999 the U.S. government downgraded the peregrine's federal status from **endangered** to threatened. In the United Kingdom, the Royal Society for the Protection of Birds no longer considers the peregrine to be a **species** needing protection.

*This Australian peregrine is on top of the world. As long as people look after its natural **habitat**, the peregrine's future looks brighter in many countries today.*

Not safe yet

Although today's world seems a safer place for the peregrine, many threats remain. Nests are still robbed to supply the illegal wildlife trade. Pollution continues to poison the food chain. Pigeon-fanciers have started a new campaign to have the falcons controlled. **Conservation** plans that work well in Europe and North America are less effective in poorer parts of the world. Here, the rising human population puts more pressure on the land. Laws that protect peregrines are hard to enforce and DDT is still used when safer, modern **pesticides** prove too expensive. Peregrine conservation has been a great success story so far, but things can change very quickly.

Learning from peregrine protection

The U.S. peregrine protection program has taught scientists a lot about protecting **raptors.** Their knowledge and experience has since been used to restore populations of other much rarer species, including the Californian condor and Philippine eagle. Without scientists, we would never have understood why the peregrine was dying out or how to protect it. But there is still much more to learn. In the United Kingdom, for example, just as the peregrine is returning, the hen harrier, another bird of prey, seems to be disappearing. It is very important that research into all raptors continues.

Winged warning signs

Protecting the peregrine does more good than saving just a single species of bird. **Apex predators,** like the peregrine, are known as **indicator species.** Because they sit at the top of the **food web,** the health of their population indicates the health of their whole environment. In the 1960s, the decline of the peregrine alerted the world to the dangers of poisonous insecticides. Eventually, these poisons affect people, too. By protecting the peregrine, people are also creating an umbrella of protection for a whole variety of life, including humans.

Getting involved

If you want to see wild peregrines for yourself, you need to get out and explore their **habitat** with a pair of binoculars. Peregrines often fly high up, so keep an eye on the skies and listen out for their harsh *kak-kak-kak-kak* call. It is easiest to spot peregrines near their nest sites, especially in early spring when the adults are calling and **displaying,** or in late summer when they are teaching their young to fly. Remember to be very careful on cliffs, and always stay back from the edge. In cities where peregrines breed, you may spot one perched high on a building. On marshes and estuaries, a flock of water birds taking off in alarm may mean there's a hunting peregrine about. Find out about good peregrine sites near you from your local **conservation** group or bird club, or try one of the websites listed on page 46.

An intimate view

You must never get too close to breeding peregrines. However, some places allow a close-up view of the nest through a telescope or on a video link. In Canada, the Peregrine Foundation runs popular Falcon Watch Centers at many urban nest sites. Here you can follow the birds' activities on a live television screen, and you will also find a whole range of information and activities. Every year In the United Kingdom, more than 50,000 people visit the peregrine viewpoint at Symonds Yat, Gloucestershire, to watch the breeding pair. Many urban nests can now also be viewed over the Internet through a webcam, which provides images and updates to your home computer.

At Symonds Yat in Gloucestershire, United Kingdom, many visitors come every year to watch and learn about the breeding peregrines.

Learn more about birds of prey by reading books or visiting websites. Then, you can share your knowledge with other, so that thay will also be interested in helping to protect the peregrine falcon.

Falconry displays

Falconry societies give public displays throughout the year. Many also visit schools. These displays allow you to see **captive-bred** peregrines and other **raptors** at very close quarters. You can watch their amazing flying skills and you may also get a chance to ask the falconer all about the birds.

Find out and join up

There are many good books and websites to tell you more about peregrines and other birds of prey. Better still, join a raptor conservation organization such as the Peregrine Fund, the Hawk and Owl Trust in the United Kingdom, or the Canadian Peregrine Foundation. You will learn a lot about peregrines. You may also be able to join in conservation activities, such as monitoring urban nest sites. With some organizations, you can even pay to adopt a wild peregrine. In return, you will receive information, pictures, newsletters, and regular updates about your falcon. When you join one of these conservation organizations, your money goes toward helping the peregrine.

ancestral home   home used over many years by many different generations

apex predator   animal that eats other animals and is so big or strong that usually no other animals kill or eat it

black market   trade in illegal or stolen goods

brood   family of young birds all hatched at the same time

captive-bred   born and raised in captivity

captive-release   release into the wild of captive-bred animals

clutch   batch of eggs all laid by one bird at the same time

conservation   protecting wildlife and the natural habitats of the world

courtship   pattern of behavior that takes place between a male and female animal prior to mating

display   dramatic activity performed by an animal to send a message, such as attracting a mate or threatening an enemy

down   tiny, soft feathers on a newly hatched baby bird

embryo   unformed baby bird inside the egg

endangered   threatened with extinction

evolve   changes gradually over a very long period of time

extinct   no longer living

eyrie   nest of a bird of prey

fertilize   when a male animal introduces sperm into a female animal's body causing eggs inside her to start growing and developing

fledgling   young bird ready to leave the nest

flight feathers   long, stiff feathers on a bird's wings and tail used for flying

food web   shows the order in which food energy passes from plants to animals

habitat   place in the natural world where a particular organism lives

hatchling   baby bird newly hatched from the egg

incubation   keeping eggs warm enough to survive, develop, and hatch

incubator   box or chamber in which eggs or baby birds are placed to stay warm

indicator species   species of animal whose welfare tells us about the health of the environment

legitimate   legal and correct

mantling   protecting food from other animals by spreading the wings over the prey

medieval   period of European history from about A.D. 500 to 1500

pesticide   chemicals used to kill insects and other crop pests

predator   animal that hunts, kills, and eats other animals

preen   clean feathers using the bill

prey   animal that is hunted and eaten by another animal

raptor   general term for a bird of prey

regurgitate   bring up food that has been swallowed in order to feed it to young

reintroduce   return a species of animal to an area where it was once found in the past but has since died out

roost   where a bird sleeps and rests

scrape   shallow bowl that some birds dig in soil to hold their eggs

species   group of living things that are similar and can reproduce together to produce healthy offspring

stoop   steep dive of a falcon hunting its prey

subspecies   one form of a species that is slightly different from other forms. Some species, including the peregrine, have several subspecies.

talons   claws of a bird of prey

territory   particular area an animal claims as its own and defends from others

tundra   flat, treeless zone in Arctic regions, where the ground is permanently frozen below the surface

Conservation groups

All of these groups work to help conserve all birds of **prey,** including the peregrine falcon. You can find out details by visiting their websites.

The Peregrine Fund

www.peregrinefund.org

This organization was founded in 1970 at Cornell University, in the United States. It pioneered **captive breeding** and **reintroduction** of peregrines across the country and is now based at the World Center for Birds of Prey in Boise, Idaho. It has been involved in many raptor **conservation** projects around the world.

Australasian Raptor Association

www.ausraptor.org.au/frmain.htm

The ARA was established in 1979 to promote the study and conservation of birds of prey throughout Australia and nearby regions.

The Canadian Peregrine Foundation

www.peregrine-foundation.ca

Started in Canada in 1997, the Foundation runs urban **reintroduction** and peregrine monitoring schemes, with Falcon Watch centers open to the public. It has many projects for volunteers and offers falcon adoption packages.

The Hawk and Owl Trust

www.hawkandowl.org

The Trust was founded in the United Kingdom in 1969. It is dedicated to ensuring that all European **raptors** and their **habitats** are protected.

The Royal Society for the Protection of Birds (RSPB)

www.rspb.org.uk

This is the world's largest bird conservation organization, founded in the United Kingdom in 1889. The RSPB works to protect all birds and their habitats around the world. It offers many educational and volunteer programs and has a network of bird reserves around the United Kingdom.

TRAFFIC

www.traffic.org

TRAFFIC is an international trade control proglem, with serveralinitiatives to stop raptor smuggling.

Webcams

Some websites feature cameras on peregrine nests. Live footage is available during the nesting season, but most sites also have archives and photo galleries worth visiting at any time of year.

United States

Des Moines

www.state.ia.us/government/dnr/organiza/fwb/wildlife/pages/falconcam.htm

Jersey City

www.njfishandwildlife.com/peregrinecam

Other cities with webcams include Albany, San Francisco, and Seattle.

Canada

www.peregrine-foundation.ca/webcams.html

Shows nest sites in many places including Ottawa, Leeds County and Hamilton.

Books

Collard, Sneed B. III. *Birds of Prey: A Look at Daytime Raptors.* Danbury, Conn.: Franklin Watts, 1999

Miller, Sara Swan. *Birds of Prey: From Falcons to Vultures.* Danbury, Conn.: Franklin Watts, 2001.

Wexo, John Bonnett. *Birds of Prey.* San Diego, Calif.: Zoobooks/Wildlife Education, 2000.

Index